ALPHABET & ANIMALS HANDWRITING PRACTICE WORKBOOK

THIS BOOK BELONGS TO :

Ant Ant Ant

Ant Ant Ant

Ant Ant Ant

B Bear

Bear Bear Bear

Bear Bear Bear

Bear Bear Bear

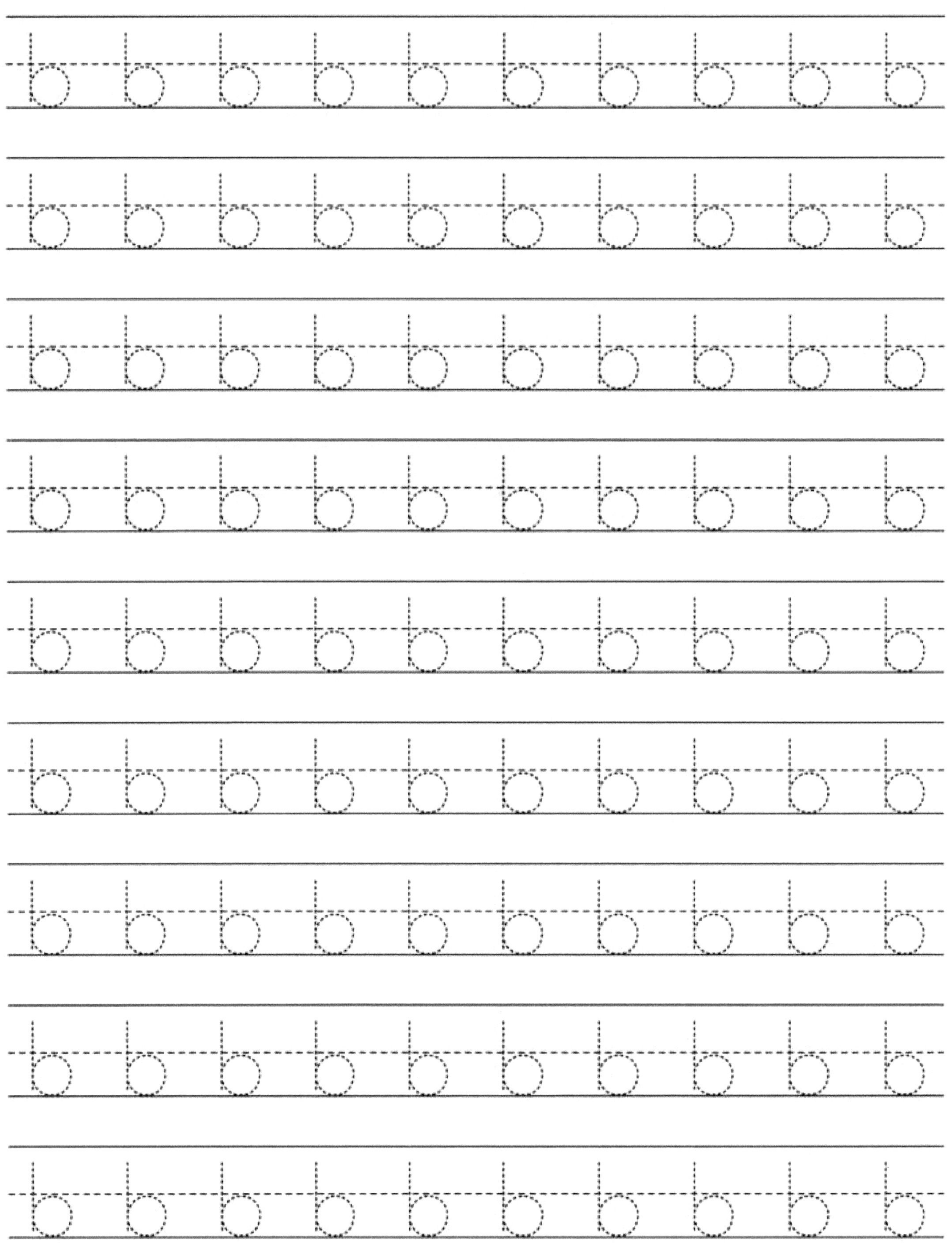

C
Cow
Cow Cow Cow Cow
Cow Cow Cow Cow
Cow Cow Cow Cow

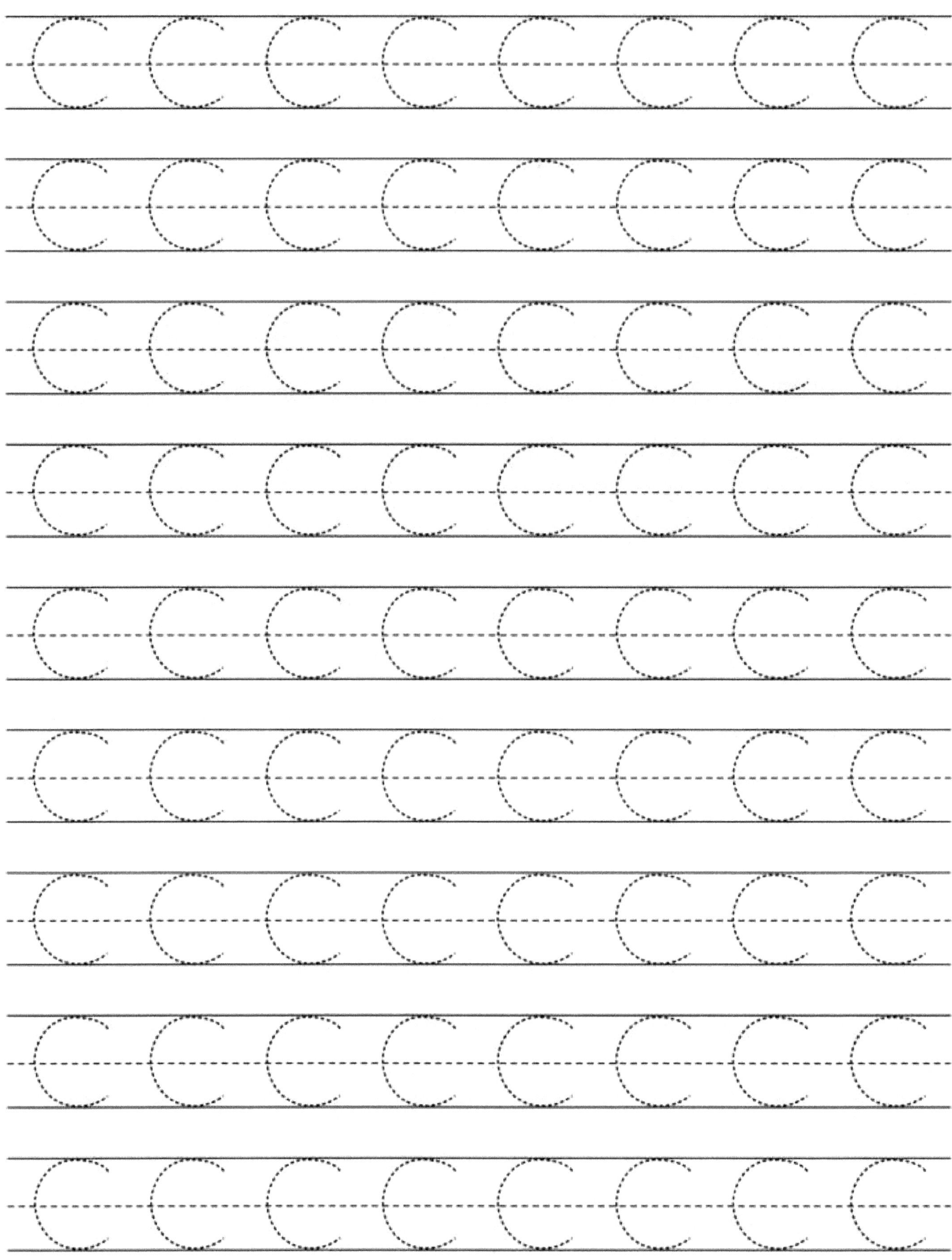

D Deer

Deer Deer Deer

Deer Deer Deer

Deer Deer Deer

D D D D D D D D

D D D D D D D D

D D D D D D D D

D D D D D D D D

D D D D D D D D

D D D D D D D D

D D D D D D D D

D D D D D D D D

D D D D D D D D

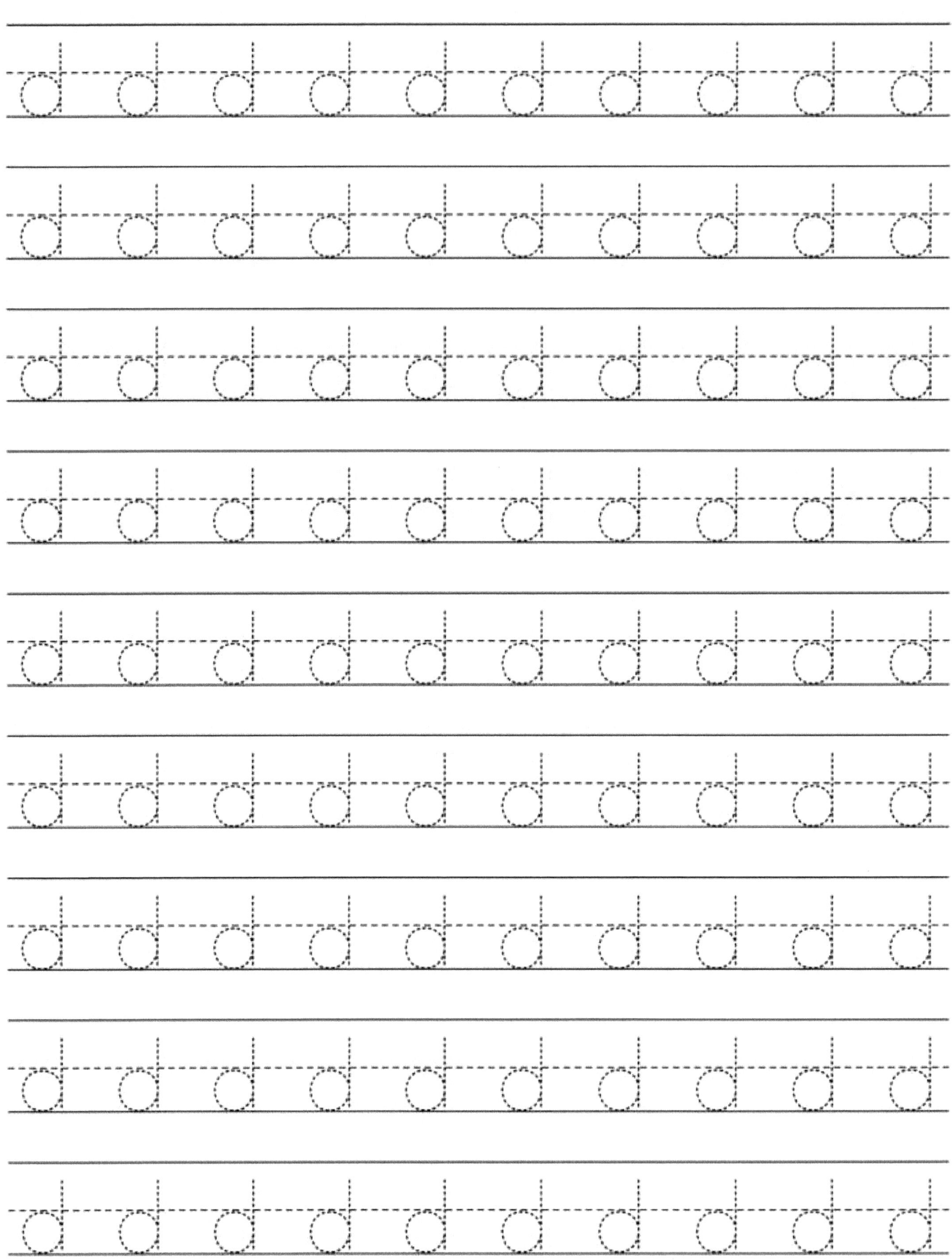

E

Elephant

Elephant Elephant

Elephant Elephant

Elephant Elephant

Frog Frog Frog Frog

Frog Frog Frog Frog

Frog Frog Frog Frog

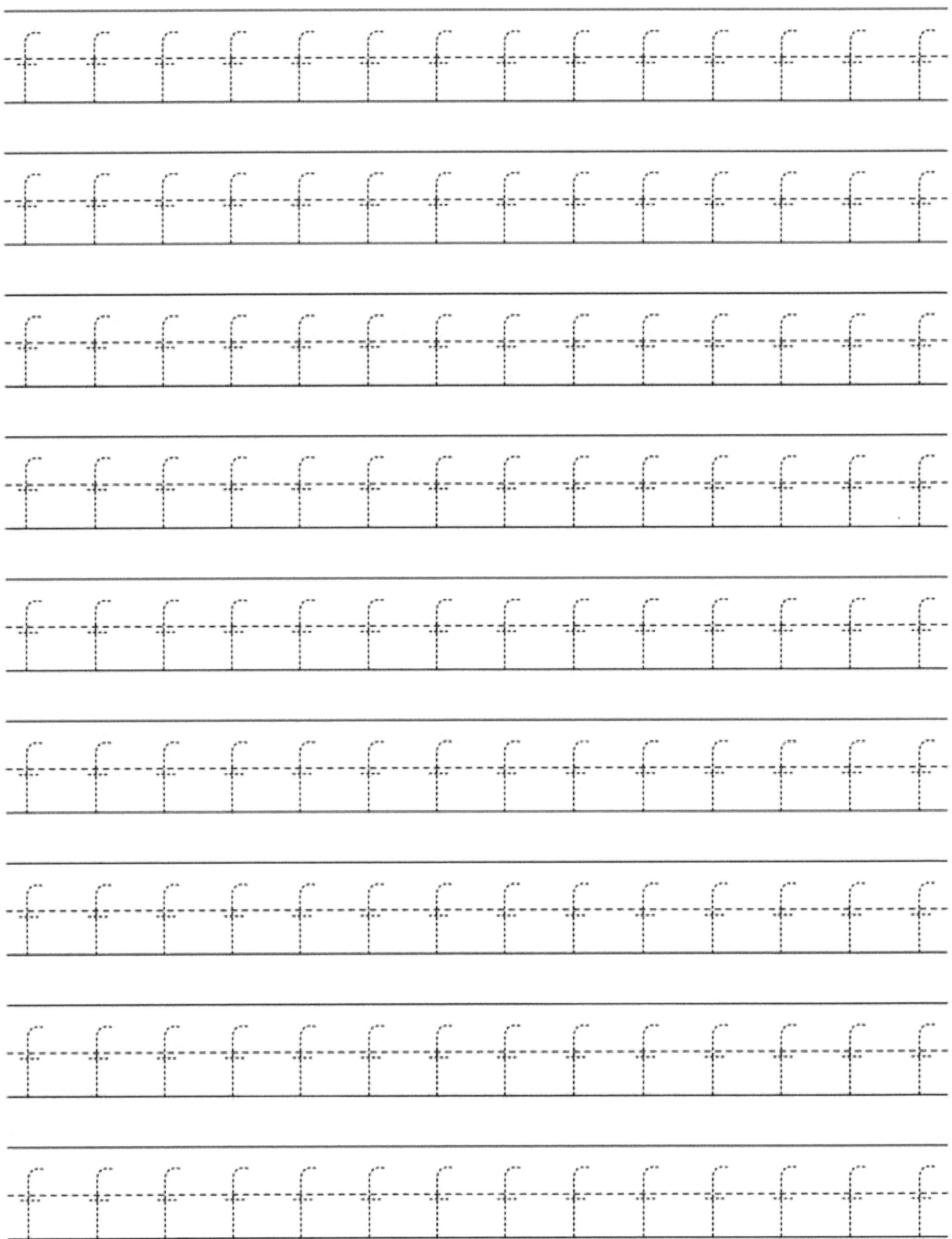

Goat Goat Goat

Goat Goat Goat

Goat Goat Goat

Horse Horse Horse

Horse Horse Horse

Horse Horse Horse

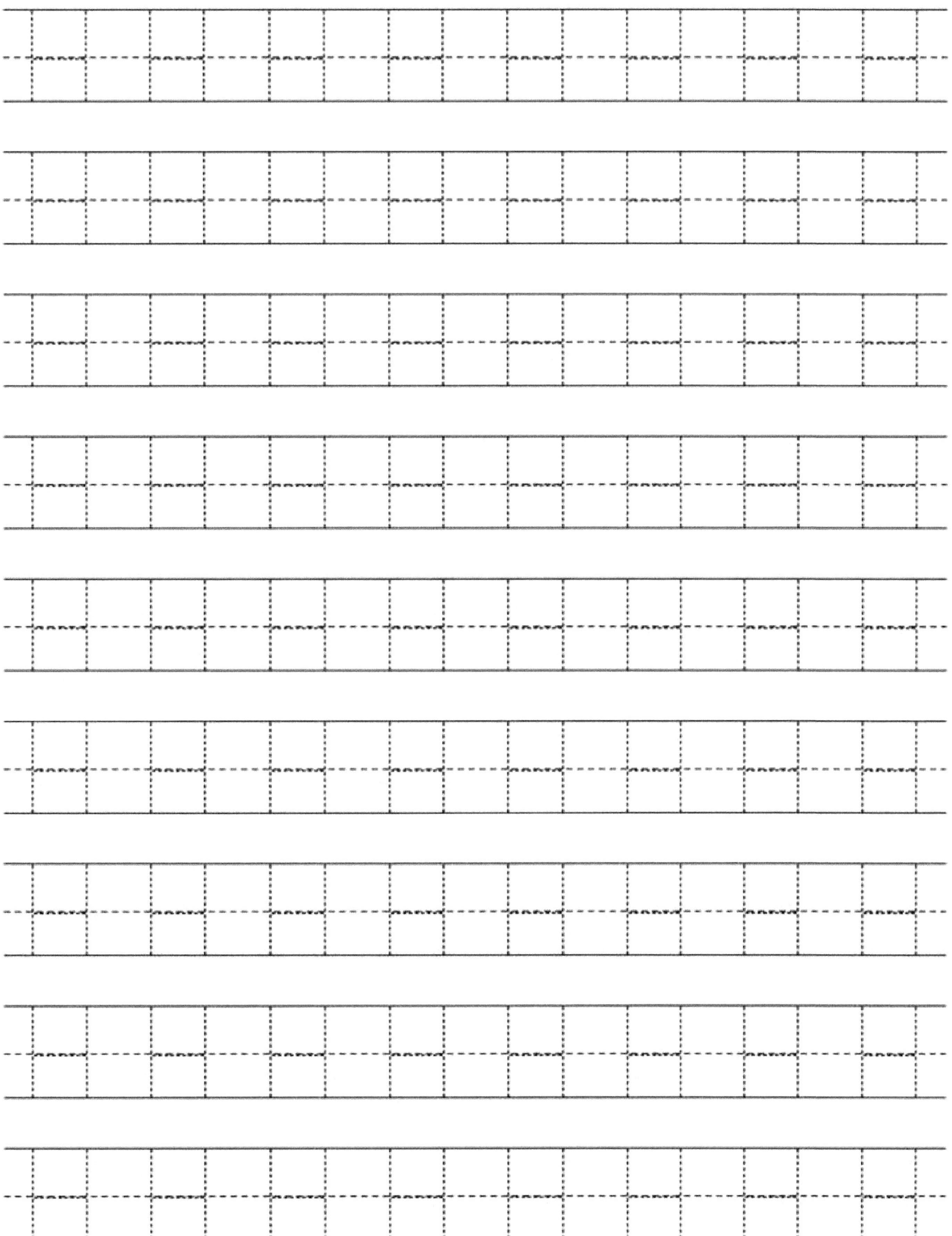

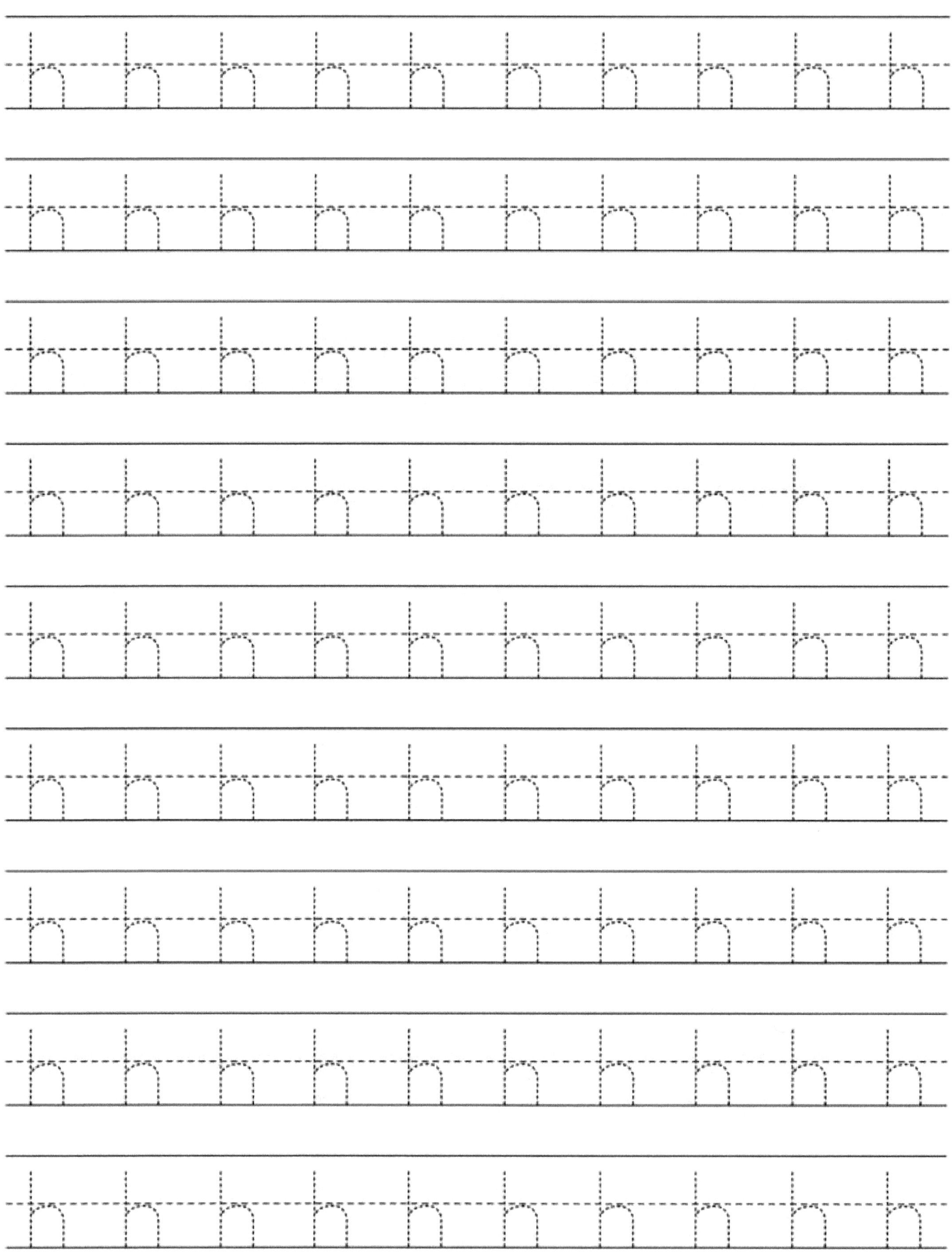

Ibis Ibis Ibis

Ibis Ibis Ibis

Ibis Ibis Ibis

Jay Jay Jay

Jay Jay Jay

Jay Jay Jay

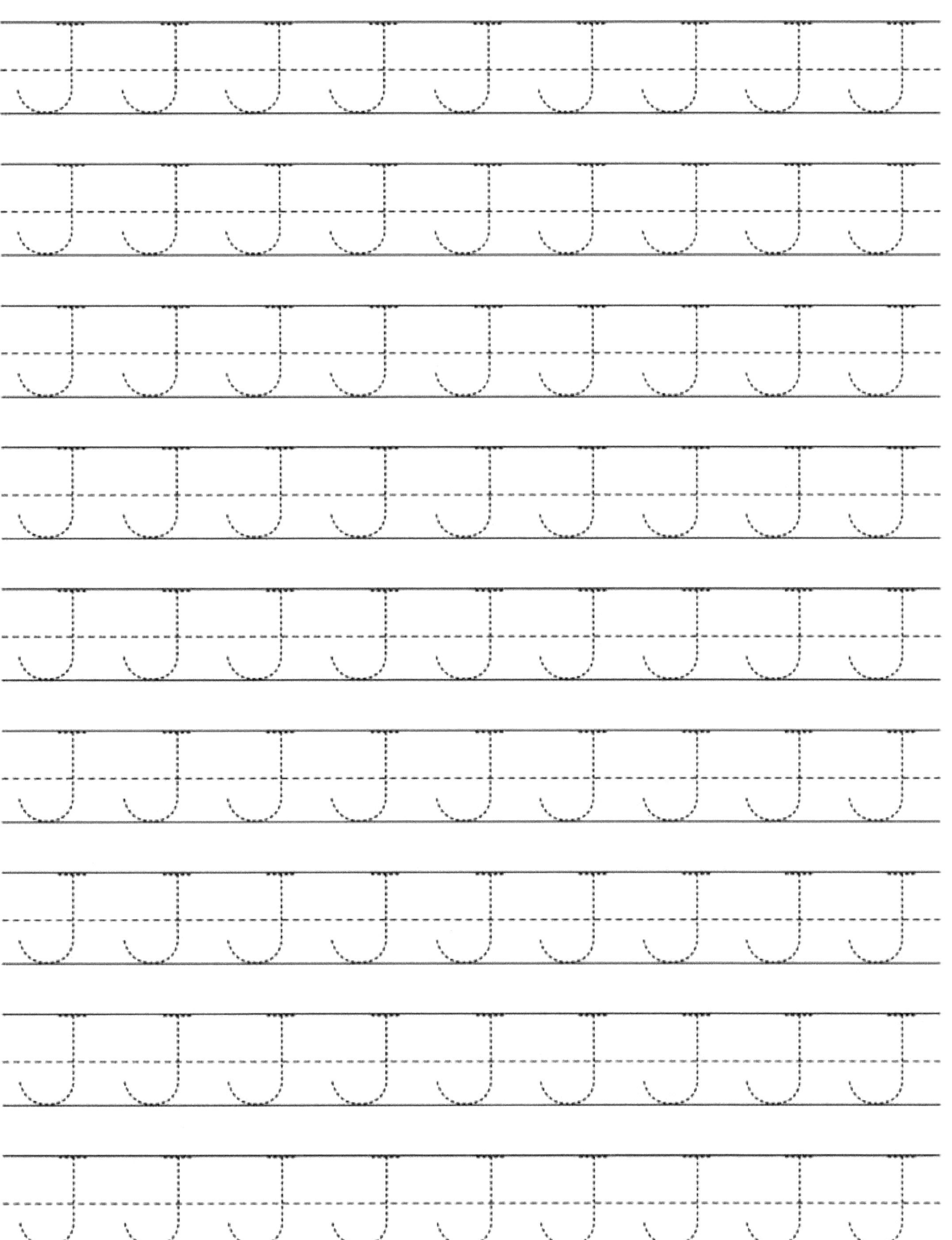

Kiwi Kiwi Kiwi

Kiwi Kiwi Kiwi

Kiwi Kiwi Kiwi

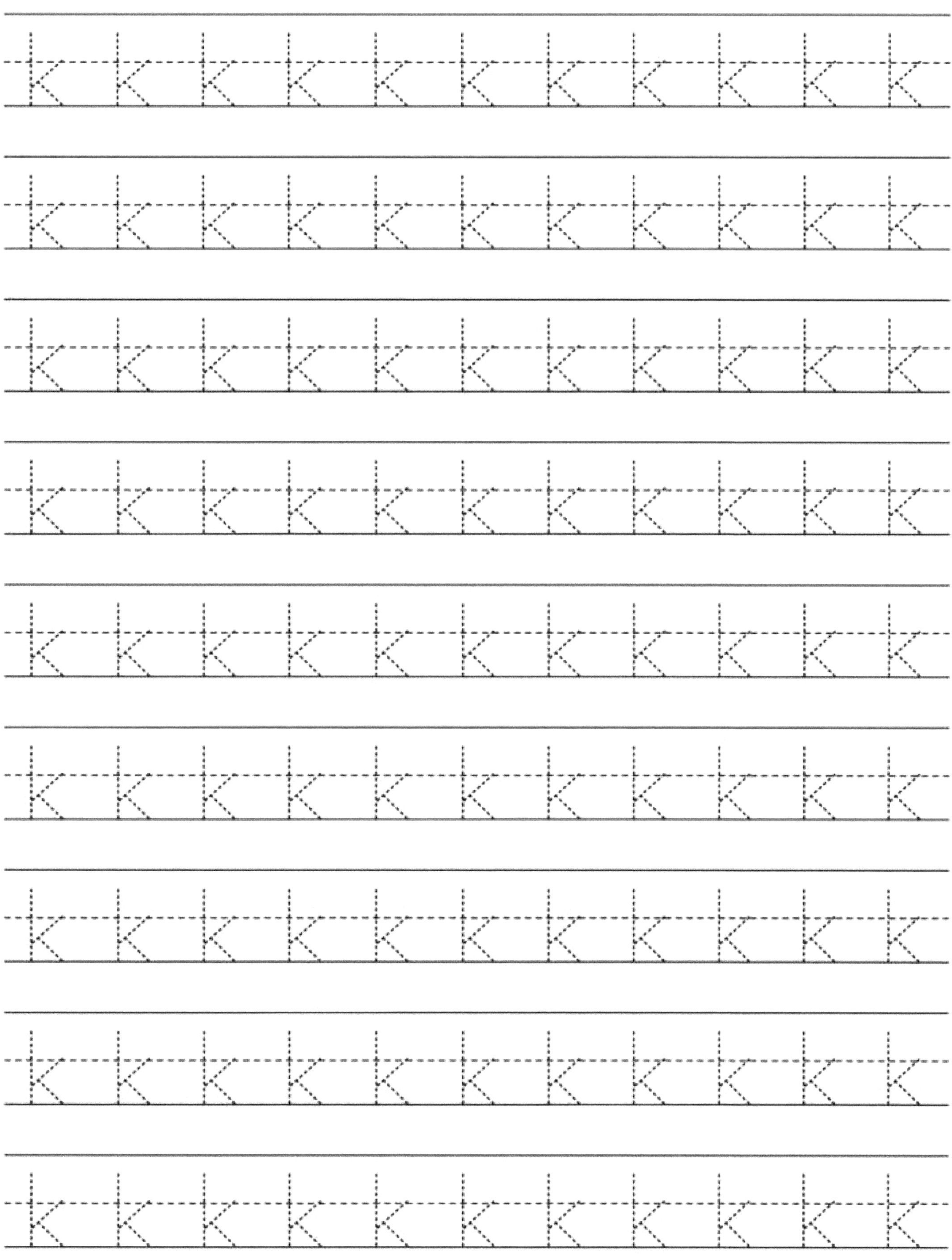

Lion Lion Lion Lion

Lion Lion Lion Lion

Lion Lion Lion Lion

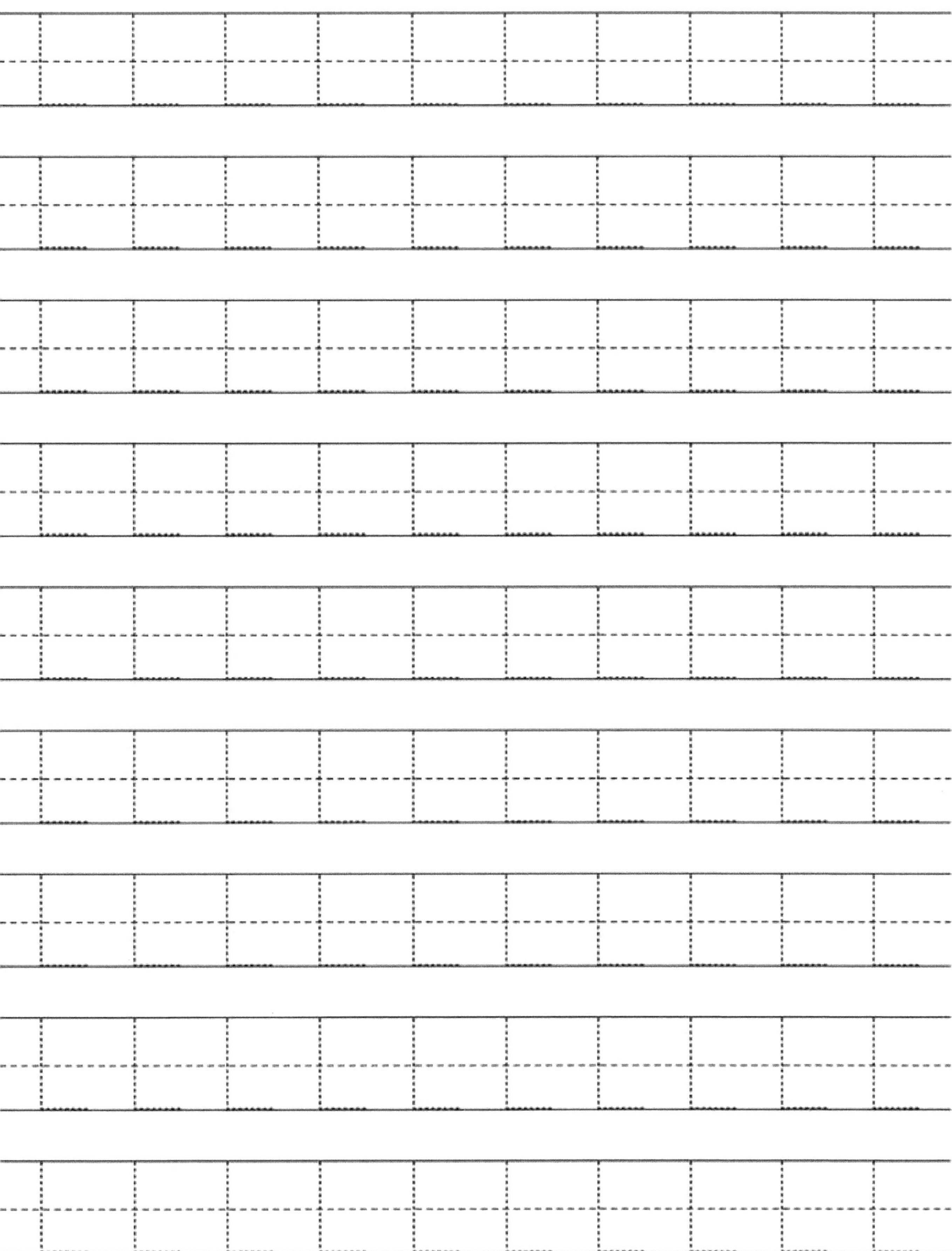

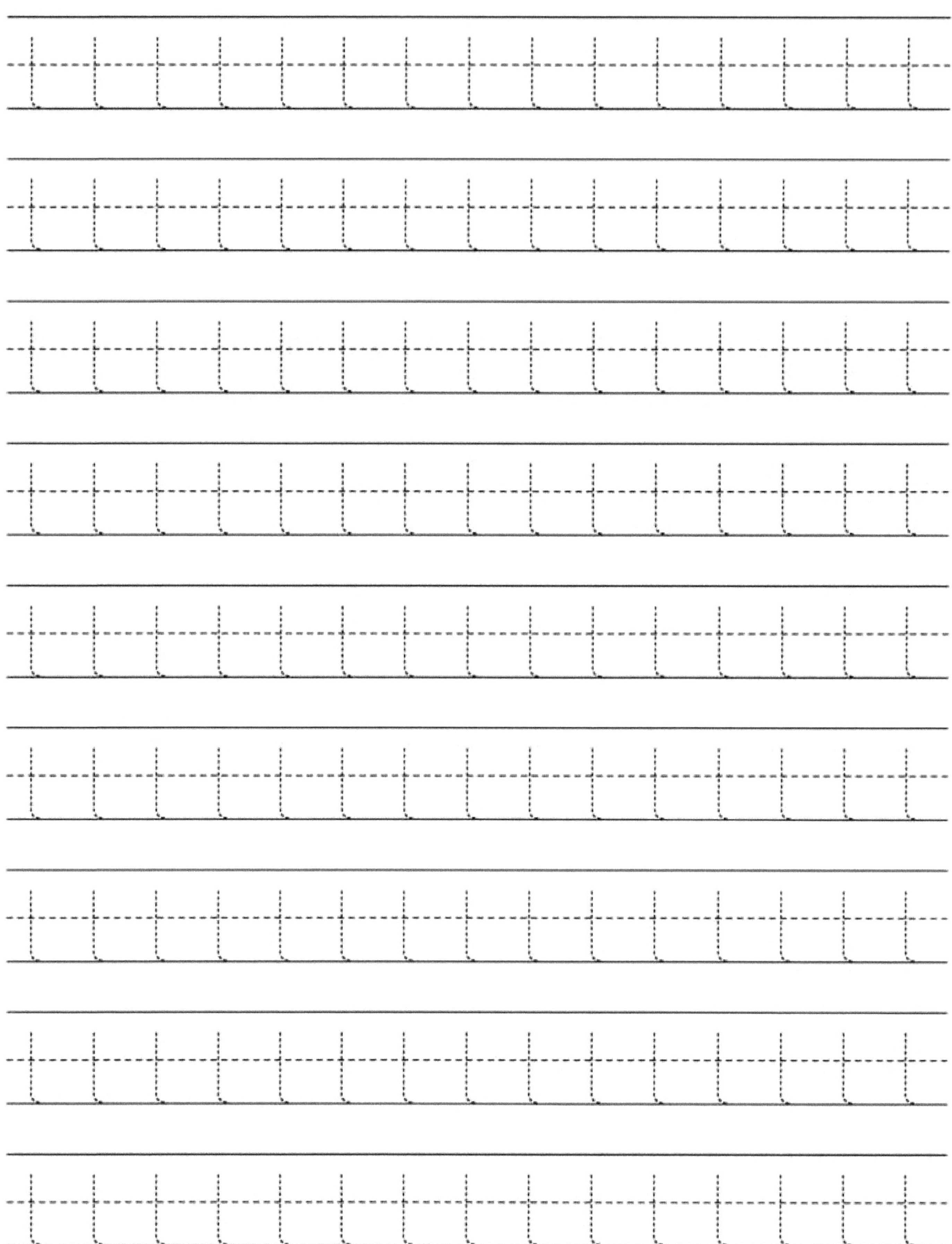

Mole Mole Mole

Mole Mole Mole

Mole Mole Mole

Newt Newt Newt

Newt Newt Newt

Newt Newt Newt

Owl Owl Owl

Owl Owl Owl

Owl Owl Owl

Pig Pig Pig

Pig Pig Pig

Pig Pig Pig

P P P P P P P P P P

P P P P P P P P P P

P P P P P P P P P P

P P P P P P P P P P

P P P P P P P P P P

P P P P P P P P P P

P P P P P P P P P P

P P P P P P P P P P

P P P P P P P P P P

Quoll Quoll Quoll

Quoll Quoll Quoll

Quoll Quoll Quoll

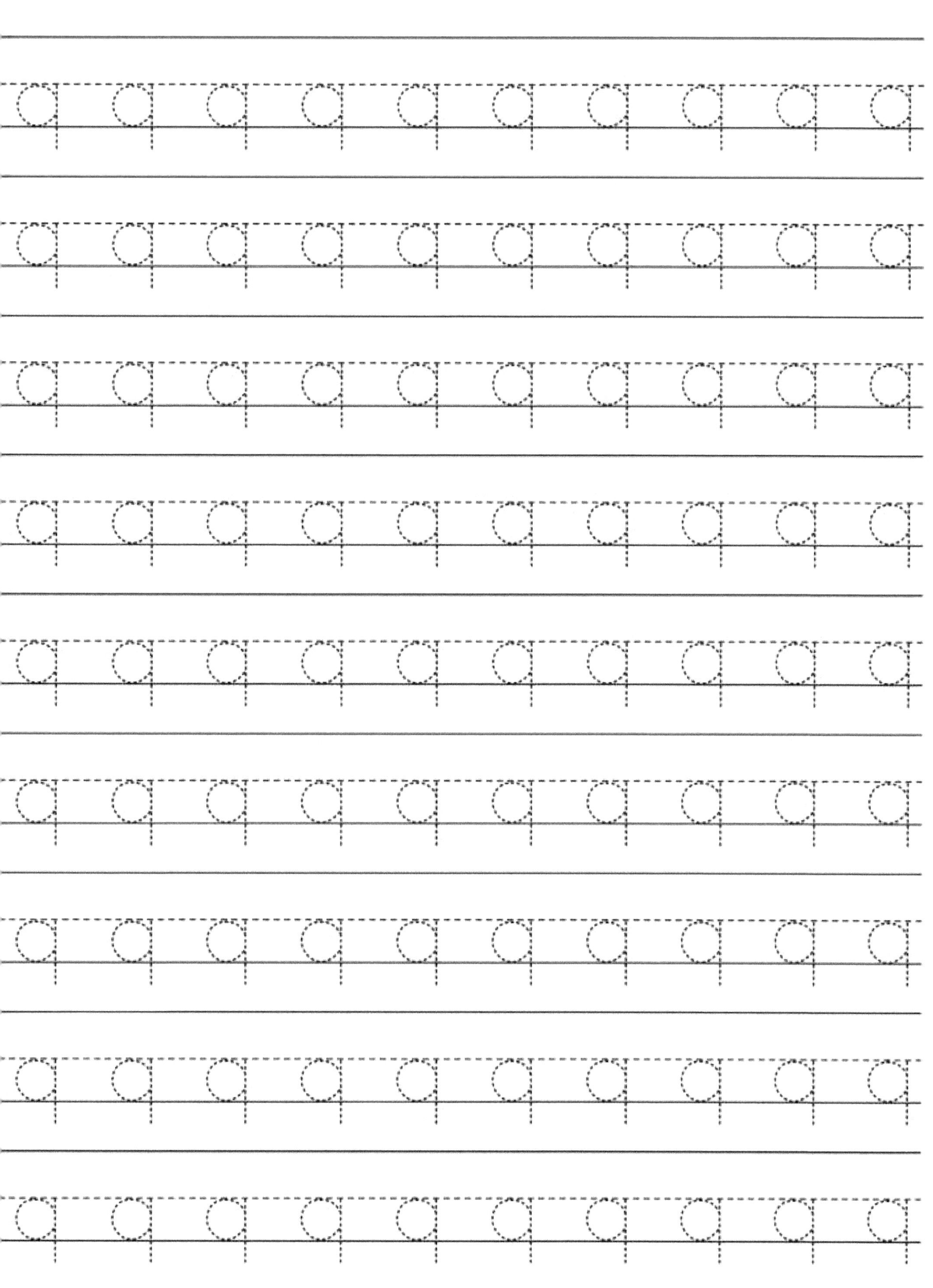

R

Raccoon

Raccoon Raccoon

Raccoon Raccoon

Raccoon Raccoon

R R R R R R R R R

R R R R R R R R R

R R R R R R R R R

R R R R R R R R R

R R R R R R R R R

R R R R R R R R R

R R R R R R R R R

R R R R R R R R R

R R R R R R R R R

Sheep Sheep Sheep

Sheep Sheep Sheep

Sheep Sheep Sheep

T Tiger

Tiger Tiger Tiger

Tiger Tiger Tiger

Tiger Tiger Tiger

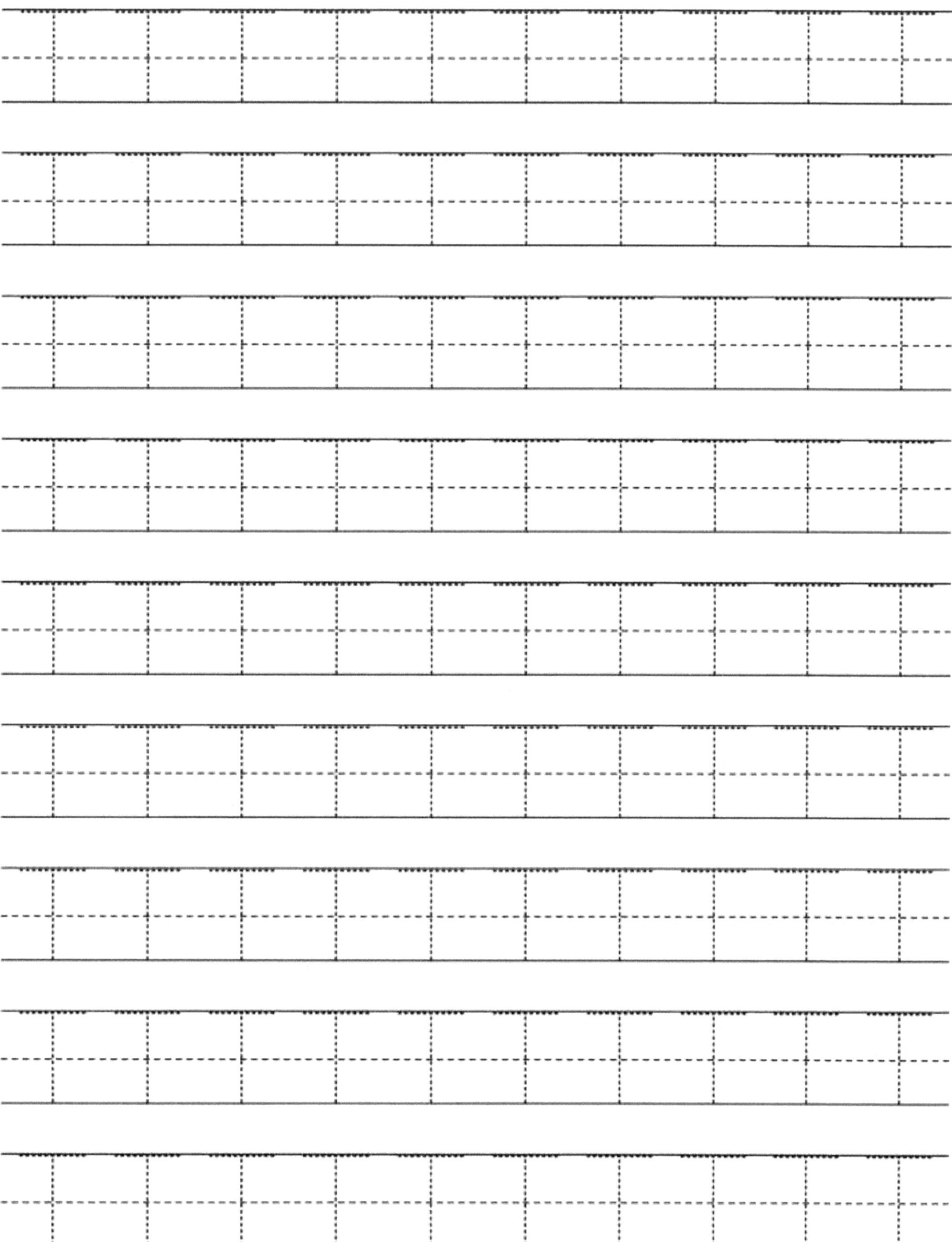

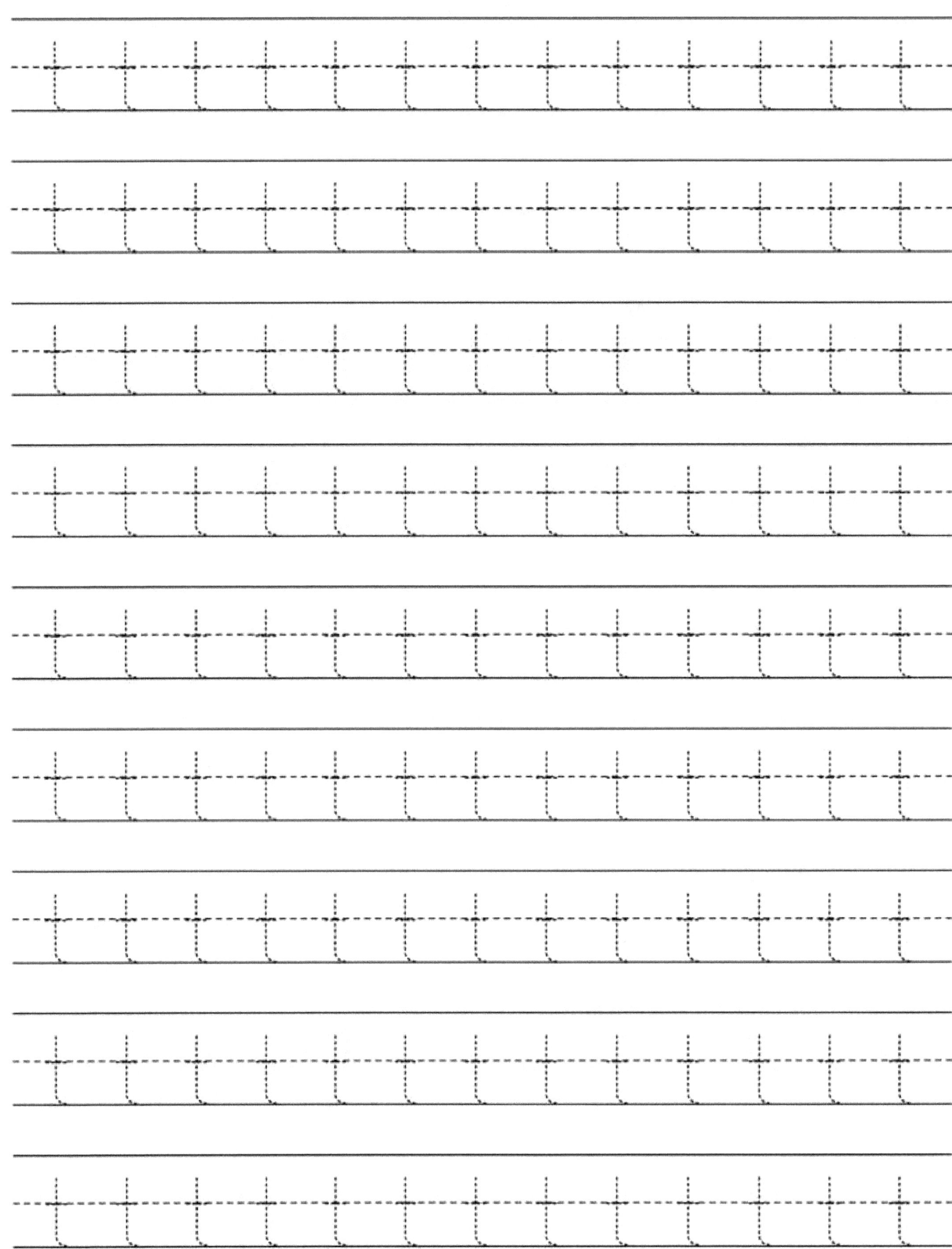

U

Unicorn

Unicorn Unicorn

Unicorn Unicorn

Unicorn Unicorn

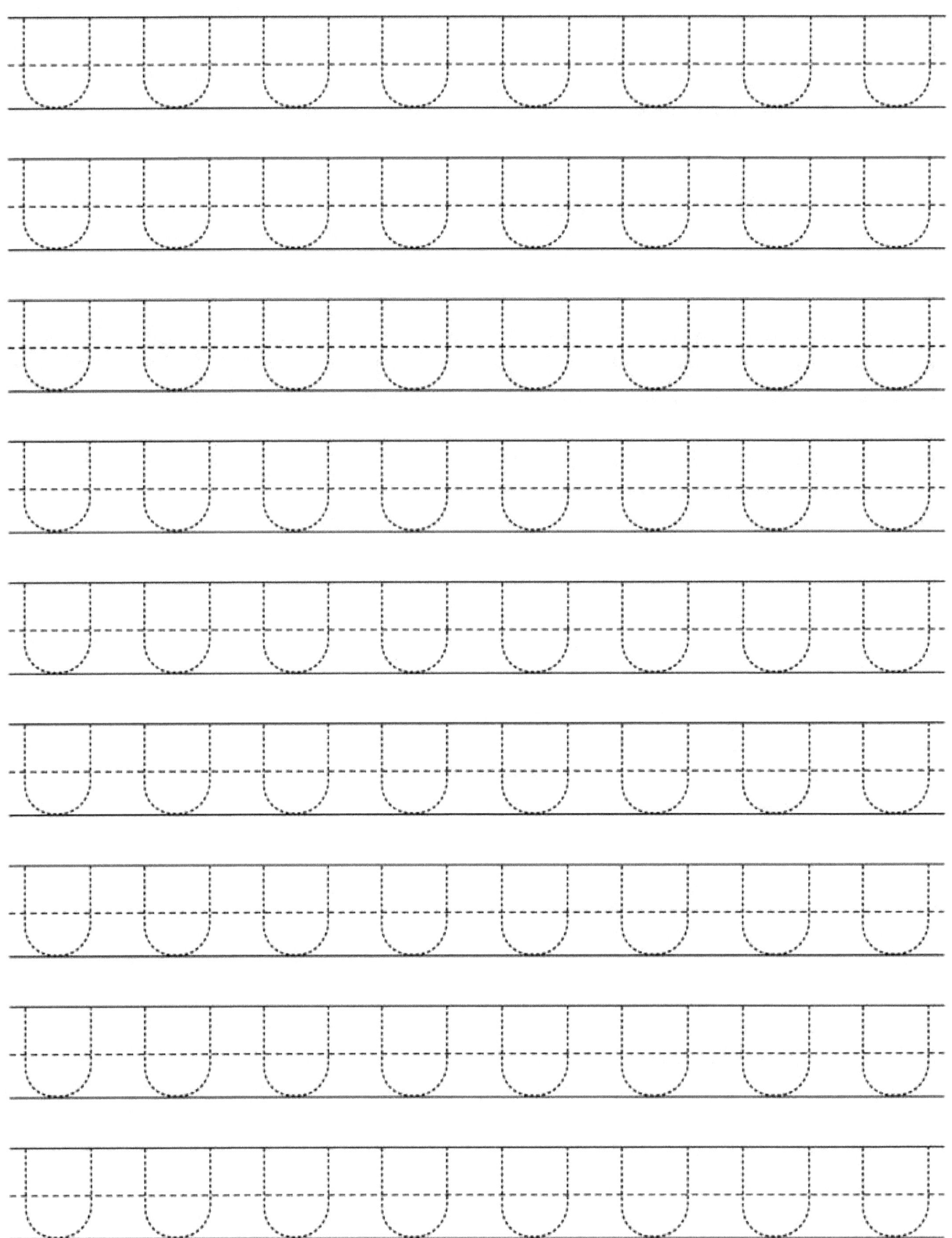

V
Viper
Viper Viper Viper
Viper Viper Viper
Viper Viper Viper

Whale Whale Whale

Whale Whale Whale

Whale Whale Whale

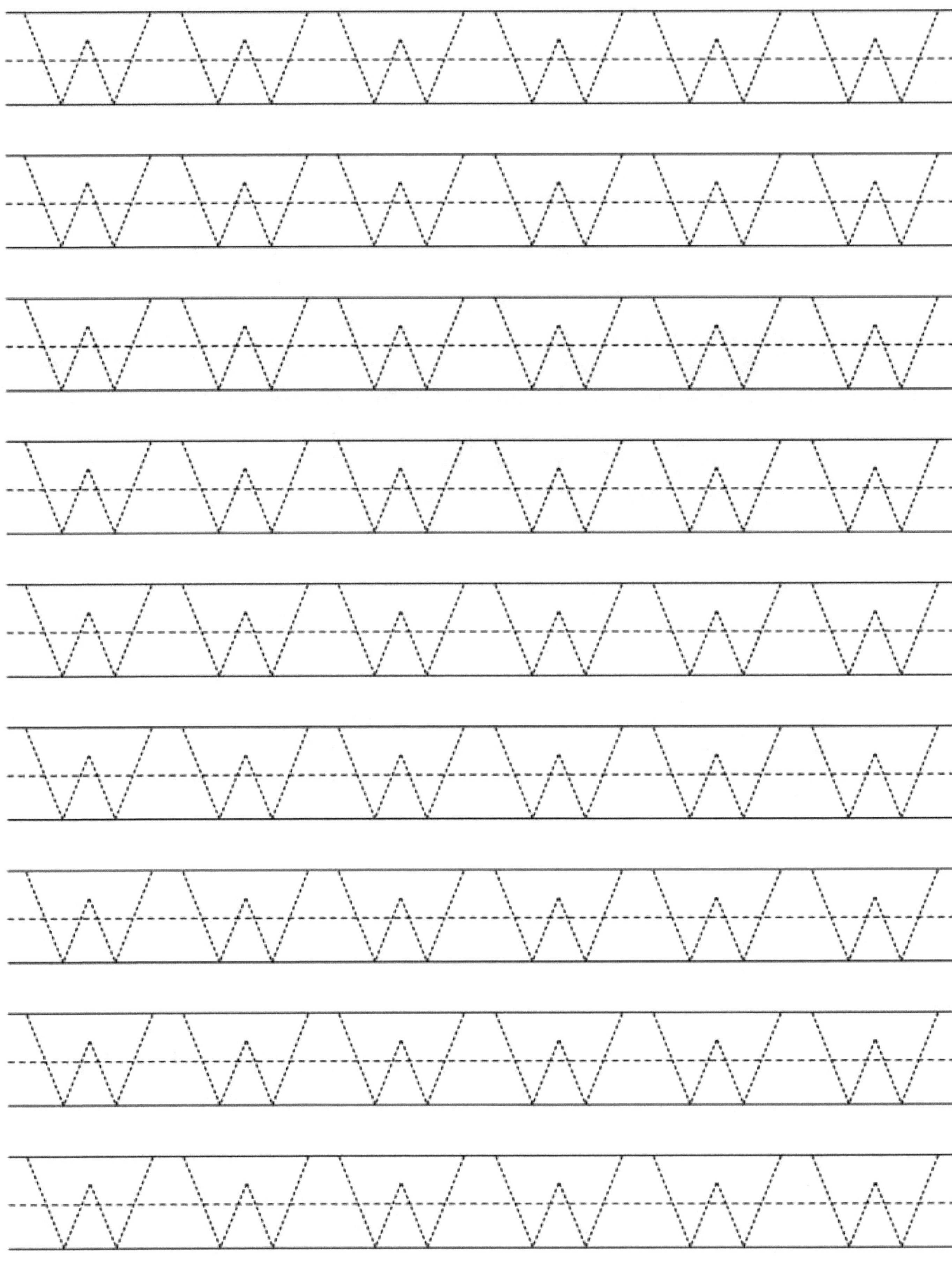

X Xerus

Xerus Xerus Xerus

Xerus Xerus Xerus

Xerus Xerus Xerus

Yak Yak Yak Yak

Yak Yak Yak Yak

Yak Yak Yak Yak

Z

Zebra

Zebra Zebra Zebra

Zebra Zebra Zebra

Zebra Zebra Zebra

www.ingramcontent.com/pod-product-compliance
Lightning Source LLC
LaVergne TN
LVHW080044170826
845677LV00024B/1599
9798716963306